KU-465-853

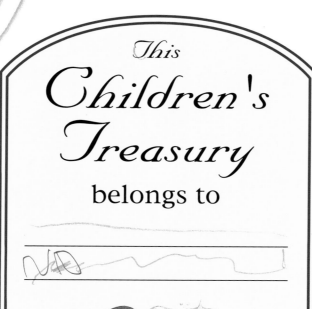

This

Children's
Treasury

belongs to

A Children's Treasury of POETRY and RHYMES

A Keepsake for Every Child

This is a Siena Book
Siena is an imprint of Parragon

Parragon
13 Whiteladies Road, Clifton, Bristol BS8 1PB

Produced by
The Templar Company plc,
Pippbrook Mill, London Road, Dorking,
Surrey RH4 1JE

This edition copyright © 1999
Parragon
All rights reserved.

Printed and bound in Singapore
ISBN 0 75252 991 9

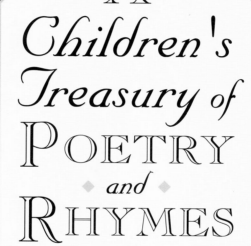

A Children's Treasury of POETRY ◆ and ◆ RHYMES

SIENA

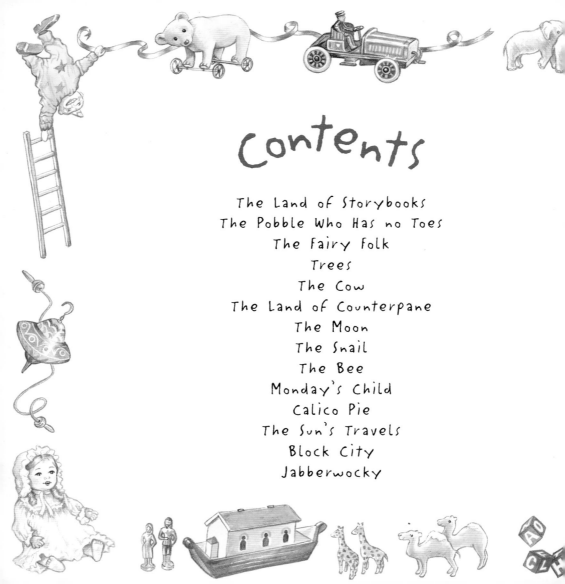

Contents

From A Railway Carriage
Turtle Soup
Baby
Picture Books in Winter
Jingle Bells
Winter Time
The Months
The Night Before Christmas
Merry Christmas
Lullaby
Twinkle, Twinkle, Little Star
Matthew, Mark, Luke, and John
Cupboard Land
Escape at Bedtime
North-West Passage
Come to the Window
Good Night! Good Night!

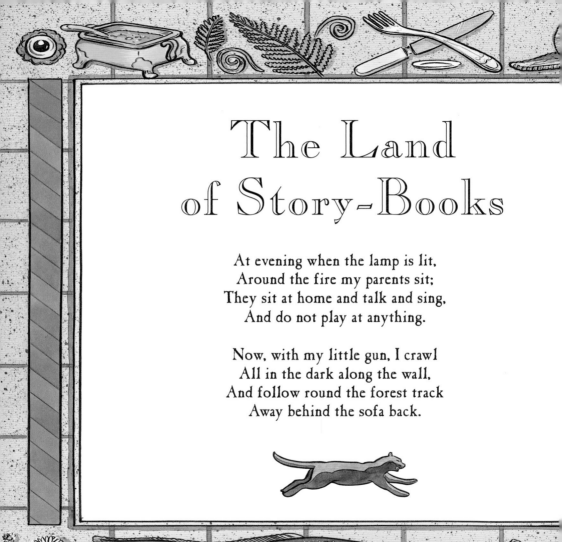

The Land
of Story-Books

At evening when the lamp is lit,
Around the fire my parents sit;
They sit at home and talk and sing,
And do not play at anything.

Now, with my little gun, I crawl
All in the dark along the wall,
And follow round the forest track
Away behind the sofa back.

There, in the night, where none can spy,
All in my hunter's camp I lie,
And play at books that I have read
Till it is time to go to bed.

These are the hills, these are the woods,
These are my starry solitudes;
And there the river by whose brink
The roaring lions come to drink.

I see the others far away
As if in firelit camp they lay,
And I, like to an Indian scout,
Around their party prowled about.

So, when my nurse comes in for me,
Home I return across the sea,
And go to bed with backward looks
At my dear land of Story-books.

THE POBBLE WHO
HAS NO TOES

The pobble who has no toes
Had once as many as we;
When they said, "Some day
you may lose them all;" –
He replied, –
"Fish fiddle de-dee!"

And his Aunt Jobiska made
him drink,
Lavender water tinged
with pink,
For she said, "The World
in general knows
There's nothing so good for
a Pobble's toes!"

The pobble who has no toes,
Swam across the
Bristol Channel;
But before he set out he
wrapped his nose,
In a piece of scarlet flannel.

For his Aunt Jobiska
said, "No harm
Can come to his toes
if his nose is warm;
And it's perfectly known
that a Pobbles's toes
Are safe, - provided he
minds his nose."

The Pobble swam fast and well,
And when boats or ships
came near him
He tinkledy-binkledy-
winkled a bell,
So that all the world
could hear him.

And all the Sailors and
Admirals cried,
When they saw him nearing
the further side, –
"He has gone to fish,
for his Aunt Jobiska's
Runcible Cat with crimson
whiskers!"

But before he touched
the shore,
The shore of the Bristol
Channel,
A sea-green Porpoise
carried away
His wrapper of scarlet flannel.

And when he came
to observe his feet,
Formerly garnished
with toes so neat,
His face at once
became forlorn
On perceiving that
all his toes were gone!

And nobody ever knew
From that dark day to
the present,
Who so had taken
the Pobble's toes,
In a manner so far
from pleasant.

Whether the shrimps or
crawfish gray,
Or crafty Mermaids stole
them away –
Nobody knew;
and nobody knows
How the Pobble was robbed
of his twice five toes!

The Pobble who has no toes
Was placed in a
friendly Bark,
And they rowed him back,
and carried him up,
To his Aunt Jobiska's Park.

And she made him a feast
at his earnest wish
Of eggs and buttercups
fried with fish; –
And she said, – "It's a fact
the whole world knows,
That Pobbles are happier
without their toes."

EDWARD LEAR

The Fairy Folk

Come cuddle close in daddy's coat
Beside the fire so bright,
And hear about the fairy folk
That wander in the night.
For when the stars are shining clear,
And all the world is still,
They float across the silver moon
From hill to cloudy hill.

Their caps of red, their cloaks of green,
  Are hung with silver bells,
And when they're shaken with the wind,
  Their merry ringing swells.
And riding on the crimson moths
  With black spots on their wings,
They guide them down the purple sky
  With golden bridle rings.

They love to visit girls and boys
  To see how sweet they sleep,
To stand beside their cosy cots
  And at their faces peep.
For in the whole of fairy land
  They have no finer sight,
Than little children sleeping sound
  With faces rosy bright.

On tiptoe crowding round their heads,
    When bright the moonlight beams,
They whisper little tender words
    That fill their minds with dreams;
And when they see a sunny smile,
    With lightest fingertips
They lay a hundred kisses sweet
    Upon the ruddy lips.

And then the little spotted moths
  Spread out their crimson wings,
And bear away the fairy crowd
  With shaking bridle rings.
Come, bairnies, hide in daddy's coat,
  Beside the fire so bright –
Perhaps the little fairy folk
  Will visit you tonight.

                    Robert M. Bird

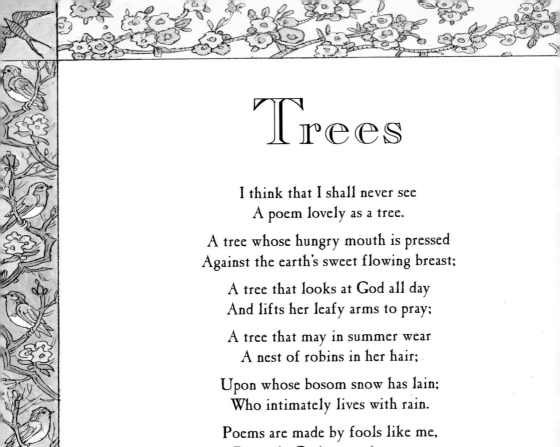

Trees

I think that I shall never see
A poem lovely as a tree.

A tree whose hungry mouth is pressed
Against the earth's sweet flowing breast;

A tree that looks at God all day
And lifts her leafy arms to pray;

A tree that may in summer wear
A nest of robins in her hair;

Upon whose bosom snow has lain;
Who intimately lives with rain.

Poems are made by fools like me,
But only God can make a tree.

JOYCE KILMER

The Cow

The friendly cow all red and white,
I love with all my heart:
She gives me cream with all her might,
To eat with apple-tart.

She wanders lowing here and there,
And yet she cannot stray,
All in the pleasant open air,
The pleasant light of day;

And blown by all the winds that pass
And wet with all the showers,
She walks among the meadow grass
And eats the meadow flowers.

ROBERT LOUIS STEVENSON

The Land of Counterpane

When I was sick and lay a-bed,
I had two pillows at my head,
And all my toys beside me lay
To keep me happy all the day.

And sometimes for an hour or so
I watched my leaden soldiers go,
With different uniforms and drills,
Among the bed-clothes, through the hills;

And sometimes sent my ships in fleets
All up and down among the sheets;
Or brought my trees and houses out,
And planted cities all about.

I was the giant great and still
That sits upon the pillow-hill,
And sees before him, dale and plain,
The pleasant land of counterpane.

ROBERT LOUIS STEVENSON

The Moon

The moon has a face
like the clock in the hall;
She shines on thieves
on the garden wall,
On streets and fields
and harbour quays,
And birdies asleep
in the forks of the trees

The squalling cat
and the squeaking mouse,
The howling dog
by the door of the house,
The bat that lies
in bed at noon,
All love to be out
by the light of the moon.

But all the things
that belong to the day
Cuddle to sleep
to be out of her way;
And flowers and children
close their eyes
Till up in the morning
the sun shall arise.

ROBERT LOUIS STEVENSON

The Snail

The frugal snail, with forecast of repose,
Carries his house with him where'er he goes;
Peeps out - and if there comes a shower of rain,
Retreats to his small domicile amain.
Touch but a tip of him, a horn,-'tis well –
He curls up in his sanctuary shell.
He's his own landlord, his own tenant; stay
Long as he will, he dreads no Quarter Day.
Himself he boards and lodges; both invites
And feast himself; sleeps with himself o'nights.
He spares the upholsterer trouble to procure
Chattels; himself is his own furniture,
And his sole riches. Whereso'er he roam –
Knock when you will he's sure to be at home.

CHARLES LAMB

The Bee

Like trains of cars on tracks of plush
I hear the level bee:
A jar across the flower goes,
Their velvety masonry

Withstands until the sweet assault
Their chivalry consumes,
While he, victorious, tilts away
To vanquish other blooms.

His feet are shod with gauze,
His helmet is of gold;
His breast, a single onyx
With chrysoprase, inlaid.

His labour is a chant,
His idleness a tune;
Oh, for a bee's experience
Of clovers and of noon!

EMILY DICKINSON

Monday's Child

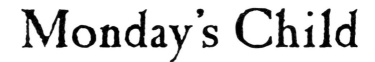

Monday's child
Is fair of face,
Tuesday's child
Is full of grace,
Wednesday's child
Is full of woe,
Thursday's child
Has far to go,

Friday's child
Is loving and giving,
Saturday's child
Works hard for his living,
But the child that is born
On the Sabbath day
Is bonny and blithe,
And good and gay.

CHARLES PERRAULT

Calico Pie

Calico Pie,
The little Birds fly
Down to the calico tree,
Their wings were blue,
And they sang "Tilly-loo!"
Till away they flew, –
And they never came back
to me!

Calico Jam,
The little Fish swam
Over the syllabub sea,
He took off his hat,
To the Sole and the Sprat,
And the Willeby-wat, –
But he never came back
to me!
He never came back!
He never came back!
He never came back to
me!

Calico Ban,
The little Mice ran,
To be ready in time for tea,
Flippity flup,
They drank it all up,
And danced in the cup, -
But they never came
back to me!
They never came back!
They never came back!
They never came back to me!

Calico Drum,
The Grasshoppers come,
The Butterfly, Beetle, and Bee,
Over the ground,
Around and round,
With a hop and a bound, -
But they never came back!
They never came back!
They never came back!
They never came back
to me!

EDWARD LEAR

The Sun's Travels

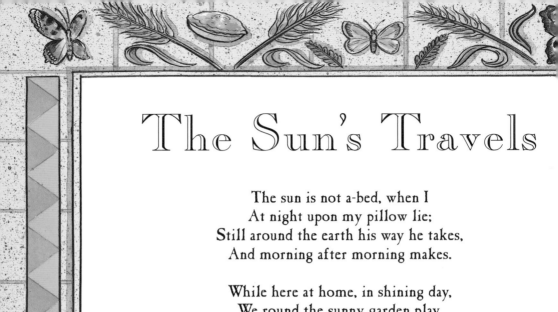

The sun is not a-bed, when I
At night upon my pillow lie;
Still around the earth his way he takes,
And morning after morning makes.

While here at home, in shining day,
We round the sunny garden play,
Each little Indian sleepy head
Is being kissed and put to bed.

And when at eve I rise from tea,
Day dawns beyond the Atlantic Sea;
And all the children in the West
Are getting up and being dressed.

ROBERT LOUIS STEVENSON

Block City

What are you able
to build with your blocks?
Castles and palaces,
temples and docks.
Rain may keep raining,
and others go roam,
But I can be happy
and building at home.

Let the sofa be mountains,
the carpet be sea,
There I'll establish
a city for me:
A kirk and a mill
and a palace beside,
And a harbour as well
where my vessels may ride.

Great is the palace
with pillar and wall,
A sort of a tower
on the top of it all,
And steps coming down
in an orderly way
to where my
toy vessels
lie safe in
the bay.

This one is sailing
and that one is moored:
Hark to the song
of the sailors on board!
And see on the steps
of my palace, the kings
Coming and going
with presents and things!

Now I have done with it,
down let it go!
All in a moment
the town is laid low.
Block upon block
lying scattered and free,
What is there left
of my town by the sea?

Yet as I saw it,
I see it again,
The kirk and the palace,
the ships and the men,
And as long as I live
and where'er I may be,
I'll always remember
my town by the sea.

ROBERT LOUIS STEVENSON

JABBERWOCKY

'Twas brillig, and
the slithy toves
Did gyre and gimble in
the wabe;
All mimsy were
the borogoves,
And the mome
raths outgrabe.

"Beware the Jabberwock,
my son!
The jaws that bite, the claws
that catch!
Beware the Jubjub bird,
and shun
The frumious Bandersnatch!"

He took his vorpal sword
in hand:
Long time the manxome foe
he sought –
So rested he by
the Tumtum tree,
And stood awhile in thought.

And as in uffish thought
he stood,
The Jabberwock, with eyes
of flame,
Came whiffling through
the tulgey wood,
And burbled as it came!

One, two! One, two!
And through and through
The vorpal blade went
snicker-snack!
He left it dead, and with
its head
He went galumphing back.

"And hast though slain
the Jabberwock?
Come to my arms, my
beamish boy!
O frabjous day! Callooh!
Callay!"
He chortled in his joy.

Hush, Little Baby

Hush, little baby, don't say
a word,
Pappa's gonna buy you
a mockingbird.
If that mockingbird
don't sing,
Pappa's gonna buy you
a diamond ring.

If that diamond ring
turns to brass,
Pappa's gonna buy you
a looking glass.
If that looking glass
gets broke,
Pappa's gonna buy you
a billy goat.

If that billy goat don't pull,
Pappa's gonna buy you
a cart and bull.
If that cart and bull
turn over,
Pappa's gonna buy you
a dog named Rover.

If that dog named Rover
don't bark,
Pappa's gonna buy you
a horse and cart.
If that horse and cart
fall down,
You'll still be the sweetest
little baby in town.

TRADITIONAL

The Swing

How do you like to go up in a swing,
Up in the air so blue?
Oh, I do think it the pleasantest thing
Ever a child can do!

Up in the air and over the wall,
Till I can see so wide,
Rivers and trees and cattle and all
Over the countryside –

Till I look down on the garden green,
Down on the roof so brown –
Up in the air I go flying again,
Up in the air and down!

ROBERT LOUIS STEVENSON

The Walru
And The
Carpenter

The sun was shining
on the sea,
Shining with all his might:
He did his very best
to make
The billows smooth and
bright –
And this was odd, because it
was the middle of the night

The moon was shining sulkily,
Because she thought the sun
Had got no business
to be there
After the day was done –
"It's very rude of him,"
she said,
"To come and spoil the fun!"

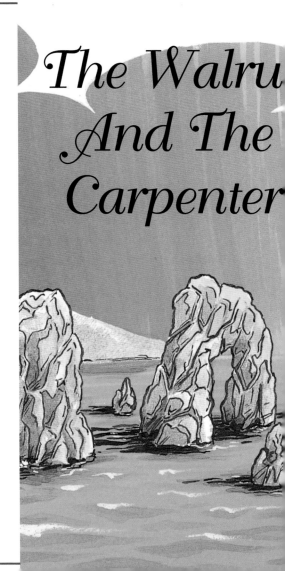

The sea was wet as wet
could be,
The sands were dry as dry.
You could not see
a cloud, because
No cloud was in the sky:
No birds were flying
overhead –
There were no birds to fly.

The Walrus and the Carpenter
Were walking close at hand;
They wept like anything
to see
Such quantities of sand:
"If this were only
cleared away,"
They said, "it would be grand!"

"If seven maids with
seven mops
Swept it for half a year,
Do you suppose,"
the Walrus said,
"That they could get it clear?"
"I doubt it," said
the Carpenter,
And shed a bitter tear.

"O Oysters, come and walk
with us!"
The Walrus did beseech.
"A pleasant walk,
a pleasant talk,
Along the briny beach:
We cannot do with
more than four,
To give a hand to each."

The eldest Oyster looked
at him,
But never a word he said:
The eldest Oyster winked
his eye,
And shook his heavy head –
Meaning to say he did
not choose
To leave the oyster-bed.

But four young Oysters
hurried up,
All eager for the treat:
Their coats were
brushed,
Their faces washed,
Their shoes were clean
and neat –
And this was odd, because,
you know,
They hadn't any feet.

Four other Oysters
followed them,
And yet another four;
And thick and fast they came
at last,
And more, and more,
and more –
All hopping through the
frothy waves,
And scrambling to
the shore.

The Walrus and
the Carpenter
Walked on a mile or so,
And then they rested
on a rock
Conveniently low:
And all the little
Oysters stood
And waited in a row.

"The time has come,"
the Walrus said,
"To talk of many things:
Of shoes - and ships –
and sealing wax –
Of cabbages - and kings –
And why the sea is boiling hot –
And whether pigs
have wings."

"But wait a bit," the
Oysters cried,
"Before we have our chat;
For some of us are
out of breath,
And all of us are fat!"
"No hurry!" said
the Carpenter.
They thanked him
much for that.

"A loaf of bread,"
the Walrus said,
"Is what we chiefly need:
Pepper and vinegar besides
Are very good indeed –
Now if you're ready,
Oysters dear,
We can begin to feed."

"But not on us!" the
Oysters cried,
Turning a little blue.
"After such kindness,
that would be
A dismal thing to do!"
"The night is fine," the
Walrus said.
"Do you admire the view?"

"It was so kind of
you to come!
And you are very nice!"
The Carpenter said
nothing but
"Cut us another slice:
I wish you were not
quite so deaf –
I've had to ask you twice!"

"It seems a shame," the
Walrus said,
"To play them such a trick,
After we've brought them
out so far,
And made them trot
so quick!"
The Carpenter said
nothing but
"The butter's spread too thick!"

"I weep for you," the
Walrus said,
"I deeply sympathize."
With sobs and tears
he sorted out
Those of the largest size,
Holding his
pocket-handkerchief
Before his streaming eyes.

"O Oysters," said the Carpenter,
"You've had a pleasant run!
Shall we be trotting
home again?"
But answer came
there none –
And this was scarcely odd,
because
They'd eaten every one.

Lewis Carroll

My Ship and I

O it's I that am the captain
of a tidy little ship,
Of a ship that goes a-sailing
on the pond;
And my ship it keeps a-turning
all around and all about;
But when I'm a little older,
I shall find the secret out
How to send my vessel
sailing on beyond.

For I mean to grow as little
as the dolly at the helm,
And the dolly I intend to
come alive;
And with him beside to help me,
it's a sailing I shall go,
It's a sailing on the water,
when the jolly breezes blow
And the vessel goes
a divie-divie-dive.

O it's then you'll see me sailing
through the rushes and the reeds,
And you'll hear the water
singing at the prow;
For beside the dolly sailor,
I'm to voyage and explore,
To land upon the island
where no dolly was before,
And to fire the penny cannon
in the bow.
ROBERT LOUIS STEVENSON

AT THE SEA-SIDE

When I was down beside the sea
A wooden spade they gave to me
To dig the sandy shore.

My holes were empty like a cup.
In every hole the sea came up,
Till it could come no more.

ROBERT LOUIS STEVENSON

Sea Fever

I must go down to the seas again, to the lonely sea and the sky,
And all I ask is a tall ship and a star to steer her by;
And the wheel's kick and the wind's song and the white sail's shaking,
And a grey mist on the sea's face, and a grey dawn breaking.

I must go down to the seas again, for the call of the running tide
Is a wild call and a clear call that may not be denied;
And all I ask is a windy day with the white clouds flying,
And the flung spray and the blown spume, and the sea gulls crying.

I must go down to the seas again, to the vagrant gypsy life,
To the gull's way and the whale's way
where the wind's like a whetted knife;
And all I ask is a merry yarn from a laughing fellow-rover,
And quiet sleep and a sweet dream when the long trick's over.

JOHN MANSFIELD

Pirate Story

Three of us afloat
in the meadow by the swing.
Three of us aboard
in the basket on the lea.
Winds are in the air,
they are blowing in the spring.
And waves are on the meadow
like the waves there are at sea.

Where shall we adventure,
to-day that we're afloat,
Wary of the weather
and steering by a star?
Shall it be to Africa,
a-steering of the boat,
To Providence, or Babylon,
or off to Malabar?

Hi! but here's a squadron
a-rowing on the sea –
Cattle on the meadow
a-charging with a roar!
Quick, and we'll escape them,
they're as mad as they can be,
The wicket is the harbour
and the garden is the shore.

ROBERT LOUIS STEVENSON

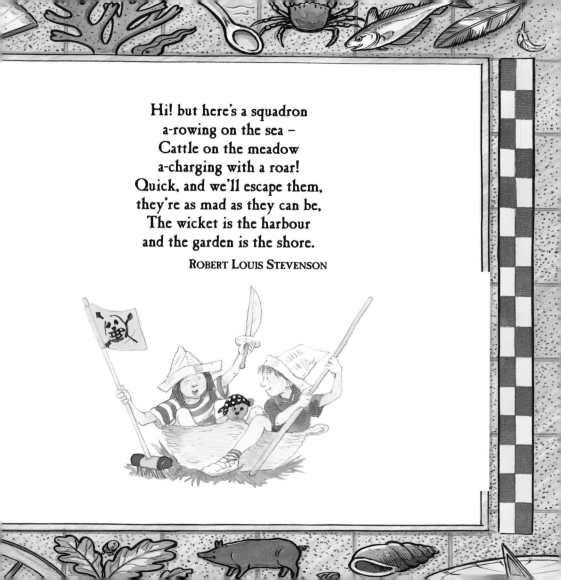

If ...

*If all the world
Was apple pie,
And all the sea
Was ink,
And all the trees
Were bread and cheese,
What should we have
to drink?* Anon

How Many Miles to Babylon?

"How many miles to Babylon?"
"Three score miles and ten."
"Can I get there by candlelight?"
"Yes and back again!
If your heels
Are nimble and light,
You may get there
By candlelight." *Anon*

My Kingdom

Down by a shining water well
I found a very little dell,
No higher than my head.
The heather and the gorse about
In summer bloom were coming out,
Some yellow and some red.

I called the little pool a sea;
The little hills were big to me;
For I am very small.
I made a boat, I made a town,
I searched the caverns up and down,
And named them one and all.

And all about was mine, I said,
The little sparrows overhead,
The little minnows too.
This was the world and I was king;
For me the bees came by to sing,
For me the swallows flew.

I played there were no deeper seas,
Nor any wider plains than these,
Nor other kings than me.
At last I heard my mother call
Out from the house at evenfall,
To call me home to tea.

And I must rise and leave my dell,
And leave my dimpled water well,
And leave my heather blooms.
Alas! and as my home I neared,
How very big my nurse appeared,
How great and cool the rooms!

ROBERT LOUIS STEVENSON

THE OWL AND THE PUSSY-CAT

The Owl and the Pussy-cat
went to sea
In a beautiful pea-green boat,
They took some honey,
and plenty of money,
Wrapped up
in a five-pound note.

The Owl looked up to
the stars above,
And sang to a small guitar,
"O lovely Pussy!
O Pussy, my love,
What a beautiful Pussy
you are, you are, you are!
What a beautiful Pussy you are!"

Pussy said to the Owl,
"You elegant fowl!
How charmingly sweet
you sing!
O let us be married!
Too long we have tarried:
But what shall we do
for a ring?"

They sailed away,
for a year and a day,
To the land where the
Bong-tree grows,
And there in a wood a
Piggy-wig stood,
With a ring at the end of
his nose, his nose, his nose,
With a ring at the end
of his nose.

"Dear Pig, are you willing
to sell for one shilling
Your ring?"
Said the Piggy, "I will."
So they took it away,
and were married next day
By the Turkey who lives on the hill.

They dined on mince,
and slices of quince,
Which they ate with a
runcible spoon;
And hand in hand,
on the edge of the sand,
They danced by the light of
the moon, the moon, the moon,
They danced by the light of
the moon.

EDWARD LEAR

Looking-Glass River

Smooth it slides; upon its travel,
Here a wimple, there a gleam –
O the clean gravel!
O the smooth stream!

Sailing blossoms, silver fishes,
Paven pools as clear as air –
How a child wishes
To live down there!

We can see our coloured faces
Floating on the shaken pool
Down in cool places,
Dim and very cool;

Till a wind or water wrinkle,
Dipping marten, plumping trout,
Spreads in a twinkle
And blots all out.

See the rings pursue each other;
All below grows black as night,
Just as if mother
Had blown out the light!

Patience, children, just a minute –
See the spreading circles die;
The stream and all in it
Will clear by-and-by.

ROBERT LOUIS STEVENSON

"Will you walk a little faster?"
said a whiting to a snail.
"There's a porpoise close
behind me, and he's treading
on my tail.

"See how eagerly the lobsters
and the turtles all advance!
They are waiting on the
shingle - will you come
and join the dance?
Will you, won't you, will you,
won't you, will you
join the dance?
Will you, won't you, will you,
won't you, won't you
join the dance?

The Lobster Quadrille

"You can really have
no notion
how delightful it will be,
When they take us up and
throw us, with the lobsters,
out to sea!"
But the snail replied,
"Too far, too far!"
and gave a look askance –
Said he thanked
the whiting
kindly, but he would
not join
the dance.

Would not, could not, would not,
could not, would not
join the dance.
Would not, could not, would not,
not, could not, could not
join the dance.
"What matters it how
far we go?"
his scaly friend replied.
"There is another shore, you
know, upon the other side.

"The further off from England
the nearer is to France -
Then turn not pale,
beloved snail, but come
and join the dance.
Will you, won't you, will you,
won't you, will you
join the dance?
Will you, won't you, will you,
won't you, won't you
join the dance?"
Lewis Carroll

Windy Nights

Whenever the moon and stars are set,
Whenever the wind is high,
All night long in the dark and wet,
A man goes riding by.
Late in the night when the fires are out,
Why does he gallop and gallop about?

Whenever the trees are crying aloud,
And ships are tossed at sea,
By, on the highway, low and loud,
By at the gallop goes he.
By at the gallop he goes, and then
By he comes back at the gallop again.

ROBERT LOUIS STEVENSON

The Gardener's Song

He thought he saw an Elephant,
That practised on a fife:
He looked again,
            and found it was
A letter from his wife.
"At length I realise," he said,
"The bitterness of Life!"

He thought he saw a Rattlesnake
That questioned him in Greek:
He looked again,
        and found it was
The Middle of Next Week.
"The one thing I regret," he said,
"Is that it cannot speak!"

He thought he saw
a Buffalo
Upon the chimney-piece:
He looked again,
and found it was
His Sister's Husband's Niece.
"Unless you leave this house,"
he said,
"I'll send for the Police!"

He thought he saw
a Banker's Clerk
Descending from the bus:
He looked again,
and found it was
A Hippopotamus:
"If this should stay to dine,"
he said,
"There won't be much for us!"

He thought he saw a Kangaroo
That worked a coffee-mill:
He looked again,
and found it was
A vegetable-Pill.
"Were I to swallow this," he said,
"I should be very ill!"

He thought he saw
a Coach-and-Four
That stood beside his bed:
He looked again,
and found it was
A Bear without a Head.
"Poor thing," he said,
"poor silly thing!
It's waiting to be fed!"

He thought he saw an Albatross
That fluttered round the lamp:
He looked again,
and found it was
A Penny-Postage-Stamp.
"You'd best be getting home,"
he said:
"The nights are very damp!"

He thought he saw
a Garden-Door
That opened with a key:
He looked again,
and found it was
A Double Rule of Three:
"And all its mystery," he said,
"Is clear as day to me!"

Lewis Carroll

Foreign Lands

Up into the cherry tree
Who should climb but little me?
I held the trunk with both my hands
And looked abroad on foreign lands.

I saw the next door garden lie,
Adorned with flowers, before my eye,
And many pleasant places more
That I have never seen before.

I saw the dimpling river pass
And be the sky's blue looking-glass;
The dusty roads go up and down
With people tramping into town.

If I could find a higher tree
Farther and farther I should see,
To where the grown-up river slips
Into the sea among the ships,

To where the roads on either hand
Lead onward into fairy land,
Where all the children dine at five,
And all the playthings come alive.

ROBERT LOUIS STEVENSON

What the Toys Do

The cupboard was closed, and the children had gone,
There were only the stars in the sky looking on;
When up jumped the toys and peeped out on the sky,
For they always awake – when there's nobody by.

The children were far away saying their prayers,
So the toys lightly stole down the shadowy stairs,
And each said to each, "We'll be off, you and I,"
For the toys - they can speak, – when there's nobody by.

So off to the city they went, two and two,
To see if, perchance, any good they could do,
To cheer the poor children whose lives are so sad,
For the toys always try to make everyone glad.

FRED E. WEATHERLY

TRAVEL

I should like to rise and go
Where the golden apples grow:-
Where below another sky
Parrot islands anchored lie,
And, watched by cockatoos and goats,
Lonely Crusoes building boats;-
Where in sunshine reaching out
Eastern cities, miles about,
Are with mosque and minaret
Among sandy gardens set,
And the rich goods from near and far
Hang for sale in the bazaar;-

Where the Great Wall round China goes,
And on one side the desert blows,
And with bell and voice and drum,
Cities on the other hum;—
Where are forests, hot as fire,

Wide as England, tall as a spire,
Full of apes and coconuts
And the negro hunters' huts;-
Where the knotty crocodile
Lies and blinks in the Nile,
And the red flamingo flies
Hunting fish before his eyes;-

Where in jungles, near and far,
Man-devouring tigers are,
Lying close and giving ear
Lest the hunt be drawing near,
Or a comer-by be seen
Swinging in a palanquin;-
Where among the desert sands
Some deserted city stands,
All its children, sweep and prince,
Grown to manhood ages since,
Not a foot in street or house,

Not a stir of child or mouse,
And when kindly falls the night,
In all the town no spark of light.
There I'll come when I'm a man
With a camel caravan;
Light a fire in the gloom
Of some dusty dining room;
See the pictures on the walls,
Heroes, fights and festivals;
And in a corner find the toys
Of the old Egyptian boys.

ROBERT LOUIS STEVENSON

THE DUCK AND THE KANGAROO

Said the Duck
to the Kangaroo,
"Good gracious!
How you hop!
Over the fields
and the water too,
As if you never would stop!

"My life is a bore
in this nasty pond,
And I long to go out
in the world beyond!
I wish I could hop like you!"
Said the Duck
to the Kangaroo.

"I would sit quite still, and
say nothing but 'Quack,'
The whole of the long
day through!

"And we'd go to the Dee,
and the Jelly Bo Lee,
Over the land, and over
the sea; –
Please take me a ride! O do!"
Said the Duck
to the Kangaroo.

Said the Kangaroo
to the Duck,
"This requires some
little reflection;
Perhaps on the whole
it might bring me luck,
And there seems
but one objection,

"Which is, if you'll let me
speak so bold,
Your feet are unpleasantly
wet and cold,
And would probably give me
the roo –
Matiz!" said the Kangaroo.

Said the Duck, "As I sat
on the rocks,
I have thought over that
completely,
And I bought four pairs
of worsted socks
Which fit my web-feet neatly.

"And to keep out the cold
I've bought a cloak,
And every day
a cigar I'll smoke,
All to follow my own dear true
Love of a Kangaroo!"

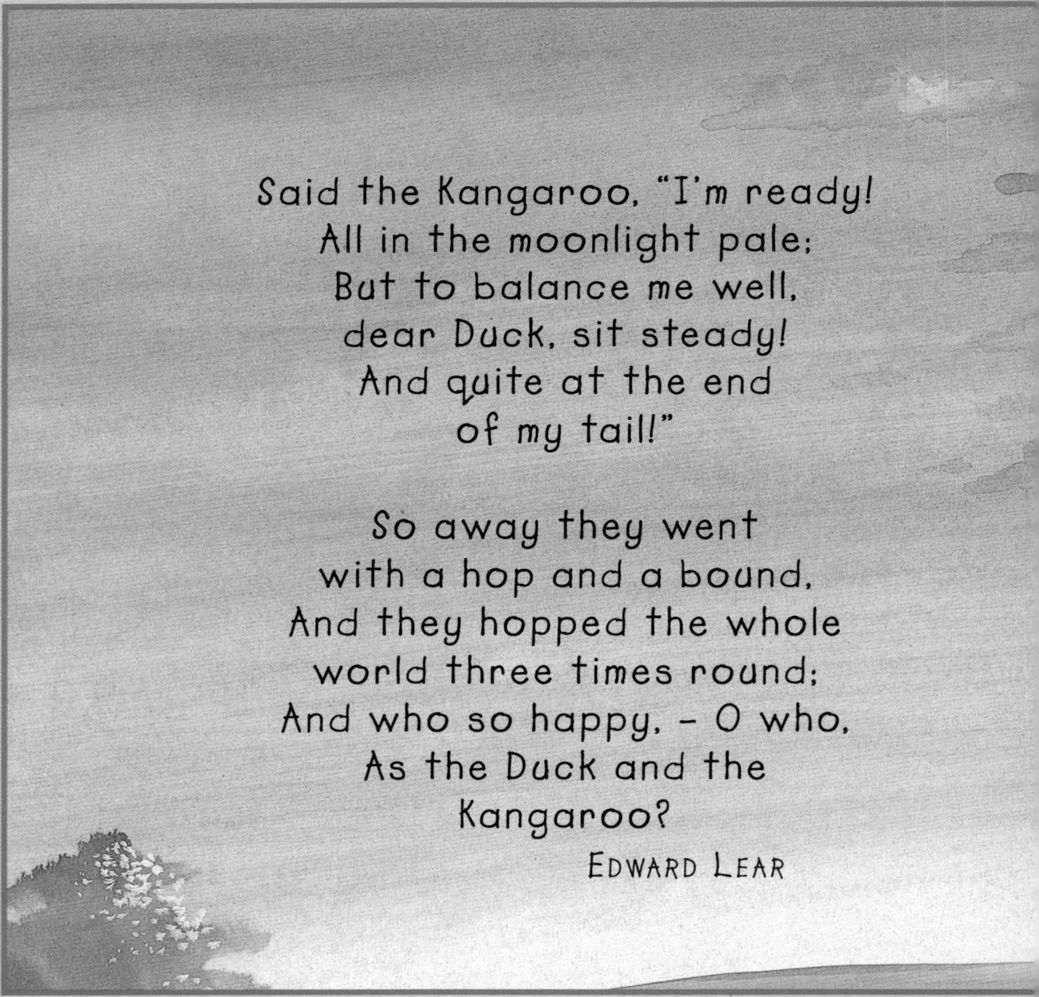

Said the Kangaroo, "I'm ready!
All in the moonlight pale;
But to balance me well,
dear Duck, sit steady!
And quite at the end
of my tail!"

So away they went
with a hop and a bound,
And they hopped the whole
world three times round;
And who so happy, – O who,
As the Duck and the
Kangaroo?

EDWARD LEAR

The
Pied Piper of Hamelin

Hamelin Town's in Brunswick,
By famous Hanover city;
The River Weser, deep and wide,
Washes its walls on the southern side;
A pleasanter spot you never spied:
But, when begins my ditty,
Almost five hundred years ago,
To see the townsfolk suffer so,
From vermin, was a pity.

Rats!

They fought the dogs and
killed the cats,
And bit the babies in the cradles,
And ate the cheeses out of the vats,
And licked the soup from the
cooks' own ladles,

Split open the kegs of salted sprats,
Made nests inside men's Sunday hats,
And even spoiled the women's chats,
By drowning their speaking
With shrieking and squeaking
In fifty different sharps and flats.

At last the people in a body
To the Town Hall came
flocking:
"'Tis clear," cried they,
"our Mayor's a noddy;
And as for our Corporation –
shocking

To think we buy gowns
lined with ermine
For dolts that can't or won't
determine
What's best to rid us of our
vermin!

You hope, because you're old
and obese,
To find the furry civic robe ease!
Rouse up, sirs! Give your brains
a racking
To find the remedy we're lacking,
Or, sure as fate, we'll send
you packing!"
At this the Mayor and
Corporation
Quaked with a mighty
consternation.

An hour they sat in council;
At length the Mayor broke silence:
"For a guilder I'd my ermine
gown sell –
I wish I were a mile hence!
It's easy to bid one rack one's brain –
I'm sure my poor head aches again,
I've scratched it so, and all in vain.
Oh, for a trap, a trap, a trap!"

Just as he said this, what should hap
At the chamber door, but a gentle tap.
"Bless us!" cried the Mayor,
"what's that?"
(With the Corporation as he sat,
Looking little though wondrous fat;

Nor brighter was his eye, nor moister
Than a too-long-opened oyster,
Save when at noon his paunch
grew mutinous
For a plate of turtle green and
glutinous.)
"Only a scraping of shoes on the mat!
Anything like the sound of a rat
Makes my heart go pit-a-pat!"

"Come in!" the Mayor cried,
looking bigger,
And in did come the
strangest figure!
His queer long coat from
heel to head
Was half of yellow and
half of red,
And he himself was
tall and thin,
With sharp blue eyes,
each like a pin,
And light loose hair,
yet swarthy skin,
No tuft on cheek nor
beard on chin,

But lips where smiles went
out and in;
There was no guessing his
kith and kin:
And nobody could
enough admire
The tall man and his
quaint attire.

Quoth one: "It's as if my
great-grandsire,
Starting up at the Trump
of Doom's tone,
Had walked this way from
his painted tomb-stone!"

He advanced to the council table:
And, "Please your honours,"
said he, "I'm able,
By means of a secret charm, to draw
All creatures living beneath the sun,
That creep, or swim, or fly, or run,
After me so as you never saw!

And I chiefly use my charm
On creatures that do people harm,
The mole, and toad, and newt,
and viper:
And people call me the Pied Piper."

(And here they noticed round
his neck
A scarf of red and yellow stripe,
To match with his coat of the
self-same check,
And at the scarf's end hung a pipe;

And his fingers, they noticed,
were ever straying
As if impatient to be playing
Upon his pipe, as low it dangled
Over his vesture so old-fangled.)
"Yet," said he, "poor piper as I am,
In Tartary I freed the Cham,

Last June, from his huge swarms of gnats;
I eased in Asia the Nizam
Of a monstrous brood of vampire bats:
And, as for what your brain bewilders,
If I can rid your town of rats
Will you give me a thousand guilders?"

"One? fifty thousand!"
was the exclamation
Of the astonished Mayor
and Corporation.
In the street the Piper stept,
Smiling first a little smile,
As if he knew what magic slept
In his quiet pipe the while;
Then, like a musical adept,

To blow the pipe his lips he wrinkled,
And green and blue his sharp
eyes twinkled,
Like a candle flame where salt is sprinkled;

And ere three shrill notes the
        pipe uttered,
You heard as if an army muttered;
And the muttering grew to a
        grumbling;
And the grumbling grew to a
        mighty rumbling;
And out of the houses the rats
        came tumbling.

Great rats, small rats, lean rats,
        brawny rats,
Brown rats, black rats, grey rats,
        tawny rats,

Grave old plodders, gay young friskers,
Fathers, mothers, uncles, cousins,
Cocking tails and pricking whiskers;

Families by tens and dozens,
Brothers, sisters, husbands, wives –
Followed the Piper for their lives.

From street to street he piped
advancing,
And step for step they followed
dancing,
Until they came to the River Weser,
Wherein all plunged and perished!
– Save one, who, stout as
Julius Caesar,
Swam across, and lived to carry
(As he the manuscript he
cherished)

To Rat-land home his commentary,
Which was: "At the first shrill
notes of the pipe
I heard a sound as of scraping tripe,
And putting apples, wondrous ripe,
Into a cider-press's gripe:

And a moving away of pickle-tub boards,
And a leaving ajar of conserve-cupboards,
And a drawing the corks of train-oil-flasks,
And a breaking the hoops of butter-casks;

And it seemed as
if a voice
(Sweeter far than
by harp or
by psaltery
Is breathed) called out,
"Oh, rats, rejoice!

The world is grown
to one vast drysaltery!
So munch on,
crunch on, take
your nuncheon,
Breakfast, supper,
dinner, luncheon!
And just as a bulky
sugar-puncheon,

All ready staved, like a great
sun shone
Glorious, scarce an inch
before me,
Just as methought it said,
'Come, bore me!'
– I found the Weser rolling
o'er me."

You should have heard the
Hamelin people
Ringing the bells till they rocked
the steeple.
"Go," cried the Mayor, "and get
long poles,
Poke out the nests, and block up
the holes!

Consult with carpenters and builders,
And leave in our town not even a trace
Of the rats!" – When suddenly,
up the face
Of the Piper perked in the
market-place,

With a "First, if you
please,
my thousand guilders!"
A thousand guilders! The
Mayor looked blue;
So did the Corporation, too.

For council dinners made rare havock
With Claret, Moselle, Vin-de-Grave, Hock;
And half the money would replenish
Their cellar's biggest butt with Rhenish.

To pay this sum to a wandering fellow
With a gipsy coat of red and yellow!
"Beside," quoth the Mayor, with a knowing wink,
"Our business was done at the river's brink;

We saw with our eyes the vermin sink,
And what's dead can't come to
life, I think.
So, friend, we're not the folks to shrink
From the duty of giving you
something to drink,

And a matter of money to put in your poke;
But, as for the guilders, what we spoke
Of them, as you very well know, was in joke.
Besides, our losses have made us thrifty;
A thousand guilders! Come, take fifty!"

The Piper's face fell, and he cried,
"No trifling! I can't wait! beside,
I've promised to visit by dinner-time
Bagdat, and accept the prime
Of the Head-Cook's pottage, all he's rich in,
For having left, in the Caliph's kitchen,

Of a nest of scorpions no survivor –
With him I proved no
bargain-driver;
With you, don't think I'll bate a stiver!
And folks who put me in a passion
May find me pipe after another
fashion."

"How!" cried the Mayor, "D'ye
think I'll brook
Being worse treated than a cook?
Insulted by a lazy ribald
With idle pipe and vesture piebald!
You threaten us, fellow!
Do your worst;
Blow your pipe there till you burst!"

Once more he stept into the street,
And to his lips again
Laid his long pipe of smooth,
straight cane;
And ere he blew three notes
(such sweet
Soft notes as yet musician's cunning
Never gave the enraptured air)

There was a rustling that seemed
like a bustling
Of merry crowds justling at
pitching and hustling;
Small feet were pattering, wooden
shoes clattering,
Little hands clapping, and little
tongues chattering;

And, like fowls in a farm-yard
when barley is scattering,
Out came the children running:
All the little boys and girls,
With rosy cheeks and flaxen curls,
And sparkling eyes and teeth
like pearls,
Tripping and skipping, ran
merrily after
The wonderful music with
shouting and laughter.

The Mayor was dumb, and the
Council stood
As if they were changed into
blocks of wood,
Unable to move a step, or cry
To the children merrily skipping by –
And—could only follow with the eye

That joyous crowd at the Piper's back.
But how the Mayor was on the rack,
And the wretched Council's bosoms beat,
As the Piper turned from the High street
To where the Weser rolled its waters

Right in the way of their sons
and daughters!
However, he turned from
south to west,
And to Koppelberg Hill his
steps addressed,
And after him the children
pressed;
Great was the joy in every breast.

"He never can cross that
mighty top!
He's forced to let the piping drop,
And we shall see our
children stop!"

When, lo, as they reached the
mountain-side,
A wondrous portal opened wide,
As if a cavern was suddenly
hollowed;
And the Piper advanced, and
the children followed;

And when all were in, to the very last,
The door in the mountain –
    side shut fast.

Did I say all? No!
    One was lame,
And could not dance the
    whole of the way;
And in after years, if you
    would blame
His sadness, he was used to say –

"It's dull in our town since
    my playmates left!
I can't forget that I'm bereft
Of all the pleasant sights
    they see,
Which the Piper also
    promised me:
For he led us, he said, to
    a joyous land,
Joining the town and
    just at hand,

Where waters gushed, and fruit trees grew,
And flowers put forth a fairer hue,
And everything was strange and new;

The sparrows were brighter than peacocks here,
And their dogs outran our fallow deer,
And honey-bees had lost their stings,
And horses were born with eagles' wings;

And just as I became assured
My lame foot would be speedily cured,
The music stopped, and I stood still,
And found myself outside the hill,
Left alone against my will,
To go now limping as before,
And never hear of that country more!"

Alas, alas for Hamelin!
There came into many a burgher's pate
A text which says, that Heaven's gate
Opens to the rich at as easy rate
As the needle's eye takes a camel in!

The Mayor sent east, west, north, and south,
  To offer the Piper, by word of mouth,
  Wherever it was men's lot to find him,
  Silver and gold to his heart's content,
  If he'd only return the way he went,
  And bring the children behind him.
But when they saw 't was a lost endeavour,

And Piper and dancers were gone for ever,
  They made a decree that lawyers never
  Should think their records dated duly,
  If, after the day of the month and year,
  These words did not as well appear;
  And so long after what happened here
  On the twenty-second of July,
  Thirteen hundred and seventy-six!

And the better in memory to fix
  The place of the children's last retreat,
  They called it, the Pied Piper's Street –
  Where any one playing on pipe or tabor
  Was sure for the future to lose his labour.

Nor suffered they hostelry
or tavern
To shock with mirth a street
so solemn;
But opposite the place of
the cavern
They wrote a story on
a column,
And on the Great Church
window painted

The same, to make the
world acquainted
How their children were
stolen away;
And there it stands to this
very day.
And I must not omit
to say
That in Transylvania
there's a tribe
Of alien people who
ascribe

The outlandish ways and dress,
On which their neighbours lay
such stress,
To their fathers and mothers
having risen
Out of some subterraneous prison
Into which they were trepanned
Long ago in a mighty band,
Out of Hamelin Town in
Brunswick land,
But how or why, they don't
understand.

So, Willy, let you and me be wipers
Of scores out with all men –
especially pipers!
And, whether they pipe us free
from rats or from mice,
If we've promised them aught, let
us keep our promise.

Robert Browning

God Bless the Field

God bless the field and bless
the furrow,
Stream and branch and
rabbit burrow,

Hill and stone and flower and tree,
From Bristol town to Wetherby –
Bless the sun and bless the sleet,
Bless the lane and bless the street,

Bless the night and bless the day,
From Somerset and all the way
To the meadows of Cathay;

Bless the minnow, bless the whale,
Bless the rainbow and the hail,
Bless the nest and bless the leaf,
Bless the righteous and the thief,
Bless the wing and bless the fin,
Bless the air I travel in,

Bless the mill and bless the mouse
Bless the miller's bricken house,
Bless the earth and bless the sea,
GOD BLESS YOU AND
GOD BLESS ME.

TRADITIONAL

The Flowers

All the names I know from nurse:
Gardener's garters, Shepherd's purse,
Bachelor's buttons, Lady's smock,
And the Lady Hollyhock.

Fairy places, fairy things,
Fairy woods where the wild bee wings,
Tiny trees for tiny dames-
These must all be fairy names!

Tiny woods below whose boughs
Shady fairies weave a house;
Tiny tree-tops, rose or thyme,
Where the braver fairies climb!

Fair are grown-up people's trees,
But the fairest woods are these;
Where if I were not so tall,
I should live for good and all.

Robert Louis Stevenson

Dear Father, Hear and Bless

Dear Father,
Hear and bless
Thy beasts
And singing birds:
And guard with tenderness
Small things
That have no words.

Anon

What Can I Give Him?

What can I give him,
Poor as I am?
If I were a shepherd
I would bring a lamb;
If I were a wise man
I would do my part,
But what can I give him?
Give him my heart. Christina Rossetti

How Doth
the Little Crocodile

How doth the little crocodile
Improve his shining tail,
And pour the waters
of the Nile
On every golden scale!

How cheerfully he seems
to grin,
How neatly spreads his claws,
And welcomes little fishes in
With gently smiling jaws!

LEWIS CARROLL

The Gardener

The gardener does not love to talk,
He makes me keep the gravel walk;
And when he puts his tools away,
He locks the door and takes the key.

Away behind the currant row
Where no one else but cook may go,
Far in the plots, I see him dig,
Old and serious, brown and big.

He digs the flowers, green, red, and blue,
Nor wishes to be spoken to.
He digs the flowers and cuts the hay,
And never seems to want to play.

Silly gardener! summer goes,
And winter comes with pinching toes,
When in the garden bare and brown
You must lay your barrow down.

Well now, and while the summer stays,
To profit by these garden days,
O how much wiser you would be
To play at Indian wars with me!

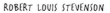

ROBERT LOUIS STEVENSON

Where Go the Boats?

Dark brown is the river,
Golden is the sand.
It flows along for ever,
With trees on either hand.

Green leaves a-floating,
Castle of the foam,
Boats of mine a-boating –
Where will all come home?

On goes the river
And out past the mill,
Away down the valley,
Away down the hill.

Away down the river,
A hundred miles or more,
Other little children
Shall bring my boats ashore.

ROBERT LOUIS STEVENSON

THE JUMBLIES

They went to sea in a Sieve,
they did,
In a Sieve they went to sea;
In spite of all their friends
could say,
On a winter's morn,
on a stormy day,
In a Sieve they went to sea!

And when the Sieve
turned round and round,
And everyone cried,
"You'll all be drowned!"
They called aloud,
"Our Sieve ain't big,
But we don't care a button!
We don't care a fig!
In a Sieve we'll go to sea!"

Far and few, far and few,
Are the lands where
the Jumblies live;
Their heads are green,
and their hands are blue,
And they went to sea in a Sieve.

They sailed away in a Sieve,
they did,
In a Sieve they sailed so fast,
With only a beautiful
pea-green veil
Tied with a riband
by way of a sail,
To a small tobacco-pipe mast;

And everyone said,
who saw them go,
"O won't they be soon
upset, you know!
For the sky is dark,
and the voyage is long,
And happen what may,
it's extremely wrong
In a Sieve to sail so fast!"

Far and few,
far and few,
Are the lands where
the Jumblies live;
Their heads are green,
and their hands are blue,
And they went to sea
in a Sieve.

The water it soon came in,
it did,
The water it soon came in;
So to keep them dry,
they wrapped their feet
In a pinky paper
all folded neat
And they fastened it down
with a pin.

And they passed the night
in a crockery-jar,
And each of them said,
"How wise we are!
Though the sky be dark,
and the voyage be long,
Yet we never can think
we were rash or wrong,
While round in our Sieve
we spin!"

Far and few, far and few,
Are the lands where
the Jumblies live;
Their heads are green,
and their hands are blue,
And they went to sea
in a Sieve.

All night long
they sailed away;
And when the sun went down,
They whistled and warbled
a moony song,
To the echoing sound
of a coppery gong,
In the shade of the
mountains brown.

"O Timballo!
How happy we are,
When we live in a Sieve
and a crockery-jar,
And all night long
in the moonlight pale,

We sail away
with a pea-green sail,
In the shade of the
mountains brown!"

Far and few, far and few,
Are the lands where
the Jumblies live;
Their heads are green,
and their hands are blue,
And they went to sea
in a Sieve.

They sailed to
the Western sea, they did,
To a land all covered with trees,
And they bought an Owl,
and a useful Cart,
And a pound of Rice,
and a Cranberry Tart,
And a hive of silvery Bees.

And they bought a Pig,
and some green Jack-daws,
And a lovely Monkey
with lollipop paws,
And forty bottles of Ring-Bo-Ree,
And no end of Stilton Cheese.

Far and few, far and few,
Are the lands where
the Jumblies live;
Their heads are green,
and their hands are blue,
And they went to sea
in a Sieve.

And in twenty years
they all came back,
In twenty years or more,
And everyone said,
"How tall they've grown!
For they've been to the
Lakes, and the Torrible Zone,
And the hills of the
Chankly Bore";

And they drank their health,
and gave them a feast
Of dumplings made of
beautiful yeast;
And everyone said,
"If we only live,
We too will go to sea
in a Sieve, –
To the hills of the
Chankly Bore!"

Far and few, far and few,
Are the lands where
the Jumblies live;
Their heads are green,
and their hands are blue,
And they went to sea
in a Sieve.

EDWARD LEAR

A-Sitting on a Gate

I'll tell thee everything I can;
There's little to relate.
I saw an aged aged man,
A-sitting on a gate.
"Who are you, aged man?" I said.
"And how is it you live?"
And his answer trickled
through my head
Like water through a sieve.

He said, "I look for butterflies
That sleep among the wheat:
I make them into mutton-pies,
And sell them in the street.
I sell them unto men," he said,
"Who sail on stormy seas;
And that's the way
I get my bread –
A trifle, if you please."

But I was thinking of a plan
To dye one's whiskers green,
And always use so large a fan
That they could not be seen.
So, having no reply to give
To what the old man said,
I cried, "Come, tell me how you live!"
And thumped him
on the head.

His accents mild took up the tale:
He said "I go my ways,
And when I find
a mountain-rill,
I set it in a blaze;
And thence they make
a stuff they call
Rowland's Macassar Oil –
Yet twopence-halfpenny is all
They give me for my toil."

But I was thinking
of a way
To feed oneself
on batter,
And so go on from
day to day
Getting a
little fatter.
I shook him well from
side to side,
Until his face
was blue:
"Come, tell me how
you live," I cried,
"And what it is
you do!"

He said, "I hunt for
haddocks' eyes
Among the heather
bright,
And work them into
waistcoat-buttons
In the silent night.
And these I do not
sell for gold
Or coin of silvery shin
But for a copper
halfpenny,
And that will
purchase nine.

"I sometimes dig for
buttered rolls,
Or set limed twigs for crabs;
I sometimes search the
grassy knolls
For wheels of Hansom-cabs.
And that's the way"
(he gave a wink)
"By which I get my wealth –
And very gladly will I drink
Your Honour's noble health."

I heard him then, for I had just
Completed my design
To keep the Menai bridge from rust
By boiling it in wine.
I thanked him much
for telling me
The way he got his wealth,
But chiefly for his wish that he
Might drink my noble health.

And now, if e'er by chance I put
My fingers into glue,
Or madly squeeze
a right-hand foot
Into a left-hand shoe,
Or if I drop upon my toe
A very heavy weight,
I weep, for it reminds me so,
Of that old man
I used to know –

Whose look was mild, whose
speech was slow,
Whose hair was whiter
than the snow,
Whose face was very like
a crow,
With eyes, like cinders,
all aglow,
Who seemed distracted with
his woe,

Who rocked his body
to and fro,
And muttered mumblingly and low,
As if his mouth were
full of dough,
Who snorted like a buffalo –
That summer evening long ago,
A-sitting on a gate.

LEWIS CARROLL

The Quangle Wangle's Hat

On the top of the
Crumpetty Tree
The Quangle Wangle sat,
But his face
you could not see,
On account of his
Beaver Hat.

For his Hat was
a hundred and two feet wide,
With ribbons and bibbons
on every side
And bells, and buttons,
and loops, and lace,
So that nobody ever
could see the face
Of the Quangle Wangle Quee.

The Quangle Wangle said
To himself on the
Crumpetty Tree, –
"Jam; and jelly; and bread;
Are the best food for me!
But the longer I live
on this Crumpetty Tree,
The plainer than ever
it seems to me

That very few people
come this way,
And that life on the whole
is far from gay!"
Said the Quangle
Wangle Quee.

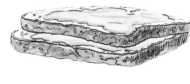

But there came to the
Crumpetty Tree,
Mr and Mrs Canary;
And they said, –
"Did you ever see
Any spot so charmingly airy?"

"May we build a nest
on your lovely Hat?
Mr Quangle Wangle,
grant us that!
O please let us come
and build a nest
Of whatever material
suits you best,
Mr Quangle Wangle Quee!"

And besides, to the
Crumpetty Tree
Came the Stork, the Duck,
and the Owl;
The Snail, and the
Bumble-Bee,
The Frog, and the
Fimble Fowl;

(The Fimble Fowl, with a
Corkscrew leg;)
And all of them said, –
"We humbly beg,
We may build our homes
on your lovely Hat, –
Mr Quangle Wangle,
grant us that!
Mr Quangle Wangle Quee!"

And the Golden Grouse
came there,
And the Pobble who
has no toes, –
And the small
Olympian bear, –
And the Dong with
a luminous nose.

And the Blue Baboon,
who played the flute, –
And the Orient Calf
from the Land of Tute, –
And the Attery Squash,
and the Bisky Bat, –
All came and built
on the lovely Hat
Of the Quangle Wangle Quee.

And the Quangle Wangle said
To himself on the
Crumpetty Tree, –
"When all these
creatures move
What a wonderful
noise there'll be!"

And at night by the light
of the Mulberry moon,
They danced to the Flute
of the Blue Baboon,
On the broad green leaves
of the Crumpetty Tree,
And all were as happy
as happy could be,
With the Quangle
Wangle Quee.

Edward Lear

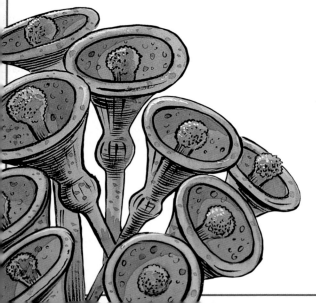

You are Old, Father William

"You are old, Father William,"
the young man said,
"And your hair has become
very white;
And yet you incessantly stand
on your head –
Do you think, at your age,
it is right?"

"In my youth," Father William
replied to his son,
"I feared it might injure
the brain;
But, now that I'm perfectly
sure I have none,
Why, I do it again
and again."

"You are old," said the youth,
"as I mentioned before,
And have grown most
uncommonly fat;
Yet you turned a back-
somersault in at the door –
Pray, what is the reason
of that?"

"In my youth," said the sage,
as he shook his grey locks,
"I kept all my limbs
very supple
By the use of this ointment –
one shilling the box –
Allow me to sell you
a couple?"

"You are old," said the youth,
"and your jaws are too weak
For anything tougher
than suet;
Yet you finished the goose, with
the bones and the beak –
Pray, how did you manage
to do it?"

"In my youth," said his father,
"I took to the law,
And argued each case
with my wife;
And the muscular strength,
which it gave to my jaw,
Has lasted the rest
of my life."

"You are old," said the youth,
"one would hardly suppose,
That your eye was as steady
as ever;
Yet you balanced an eel on
the end of your nose –
What made you so
awfully clever?"

"I have answered three
questions, and that is enough,"
Said his father;
"don't give yourself airs!
Do you think I can listen all
day to such stuff?
Be off, or I'll kick you
downstairs!"

Lewis Carroll

The Wind

I saw you toss the kites on high
And blow the birds about the sky;
And all around I heard you pass,
Like ladies' skirts across the grass –
O wind, a-blowing all day long,
O wind, that sings so loud a song!

I saw the different things you did,
But always you yourself you hid.
I felt you push, I heard you call,
I could not see yourself at all –
O wind, a-blowing all day long,
O wind, that sings so loud a song!

O you that are so strong and cold,
O blower, are you young or old?
Are you a beast of field and tree,
Or just a stronger child than me?
O wind, a-blowing all day long,
O wind, that sings so loud a song!

ROBERT LOUIS STEVENSON

As I was Going to St Ives

As I was going to St Ives,
I met a man with seven wives;
Each wife had seven sacks,
Each sack had seven cats,
Each cat had seven kits:
Kits, cats, sacks, and wives,
How many were going
To St Ives?
   Anon

A Wise Old Owl

A wise old owl
Lived in an oak;
The more he saw
The less he spoke.
The less he spoke
The more he heard.
Why can't we all be
Like that wise old bird? *Traditional*

Autumn Fires

In the other gardens
And all up the vale,
From the autumn bonfires
See the smoke trail!

Pleasant summer over
And all the summer flowers,
The red fire blazes,
The grey smoke towers.

Sing a song of seasons!
Something bright in all!
Flowers in the summer,
Fires in the fall!

ROBERT LOUIS STEVENSON

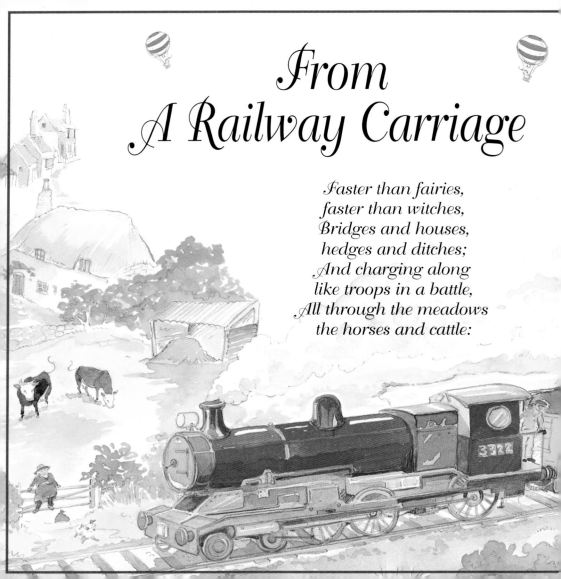

From
A Railway Carriage

Faster than fairies,
faster than witches,
Bridges and houses,
hedges and ditches;
And charging along
like troops in a battle,
All through the meadows
the horses and cattle:

All of the sights
of the hill and the plain
Fly as thick
as driving rain;
And ever again,
in the wink of an eye,
Painted stations
whistle by.

Here is a child
who clambers and scrambles,
All by himself
and gathering brambles;
Here is a tramp
who stands and gazes;
And there is the green
for stringing the daisies!
Here is a cart
run away in the road
Lumping along
with man and load;
And here is a mill
and there is a river:
Each a glimpse
and gone for ever!

Robert Louis Stevenson

TURTLE SOUP

Beautiful Soup,
so rich and green,
Waiting in a hot tureen!
Who for such dainties
would not stoop?
Soup of the evening,
beautiful Soup!

Soup of the evening,
beautiful Soup!
Beau-ootiful Soo-oop!
Beau-ootiful Soo-oop!
Soo-oop of the e-e-evening,
Beautiful, beautiful Soup!

Beautiful Soup!
Who cares for fish,
Game, or any other dish!
Who would not give
all else for two
pennyworth only of
beautiful Soup?
Pennyworth only of
beautiful Soup?
Beau-ootiful Soo-oop!
Beau-ootiful Soo-oop!
Soo-oop of the e-e-evening,
Beautiful, beauti-FUL SOUP!

LEWIS CARROLL

Baby

Where did you come from, baby dear?
"Out of the everywhere into here."

Where did you get those eyes so blue?
"Out of the sky as I came through."

What makes the light in them sparkle and spin?
"Some of the starry spikes left in."

Where did you get that little tear?
"I found it waiting when I got here."

What makes your forehead so smooth and high?
"A soft hand stroked it as I went by."

What makes your cheek like a warm white rose?
"I saw something better than anyone knows."

Whence that three-cornered smile of bliss?
"Three angels gave me at once a kiss."

Where did you get this pearly ear?
"God spoke, and it came out to hear."

Where did you get those arms and hands?
"Love made itself into bonds and bands."

George MacDonald

Picture-Books in Winter

Summer fading, winter comes –
Frosty mornings, tingling thumbs,
Window robins, winter rooks,
And the picture story-books.

Water now is turned to stone
Nurse and I can walk upon;
Still we find the flowing brooks
In the picture story-books.

All the pretty things put by,
Wait upon the children's eye,
Sheep and shepherds, trees and crooks,
In the picture story-books.

We may see how all things are
Seas and cities, near and far,
And the flying fairies' looks,
In the picture story-books.

How am I to sing your praise,
Happy chimney-corner days,
Sitting safe in nursery nooks,
Reading picture story-books?

Robert Louis Stevenson

Jingle Bells

Jingle bells, jingle bells,
Jingle all the way,
Oh what fun it is to ride
In a one-horse open sleigh.

Dashing through the snow,
In a one-horse open sleigh,
O'er the fields we go,
Laughing all the way.

Bells on bob-tail ring,
Making spirits bright;
What fun it is to ride and sing
A sleighing song tonight.

Jingle bells, jingle bells,
Jingle all the way,
Oh what fun it is to ride
In a one-horse open sleigh.

CLEMENT CLARKE MOORE

Winter Time

Late lies the wintry sun a-bed,
A frosty, fiery sleepy-head;
Blinks but an hour or two; and then,
A blood-red orange, sets again.

Before the stars have left the skies,
At morning in the dark I rise;
And shivering in my nakedness,
By the cold candle, bathe and dress.

Close by the jolly fire I sit
To warm my frozen bones a bit;
Or with a reindeer-sled, explore
The colder countries round the door.

When to go out, my nurse doth wrap
Me in my comforter and cap;
The cold wind burns my face, and blows
Its frosty pepper up my nose.

Black are my steps on silver sod;
Thick blows my frosty breath abroad;
And tree and house, and hill and lake
Are frosted like a wedding-cake.

ROBERT LOUIS STEVENSON

The Months

January brings the snow,
Makes our feet and fingers glow.

February brings the rain,
Thaws the frozen lake again.

March brings breezes loud and shrill,
Stirs the dancing daffodil.

April brings the primrose sweet,
Scatters daisies at our feet.

May brings flocks of pretty lambs,
Skipping by their fleecy dams.

June brings tulips, lilies, roses,
Fills the children's hands with posies.

Hot July brings cooling showers,
Apricots and gillyflowers.

August brings the sheaves of corn,
Then the harvest home is borne.

Warm September brings the fruit,
Sportsmen then begin to shoot.

Fresh October brings the pheasant,
Then to gather nuts is pleasant.

Dull November brings the blast,
Then the leaves are whirling fast.

Chill December brings the sleet,
Blazing fire and Christmas treat!

SARA COLERIDGE

The
Night Before Christmas

'*T*was the night before Christmas,
when all through the house
Not a creature was stirring,
not even a mouse;

The stockings were hung
by the chimney with care,
In hopes that St. Nicholas
soon would be there;

The children were nestled
all snug in their beds
While visions of sugar plums
danced in their heads;

And Mamma in her kerchief,
and I in my cap,
Had just settled our brains
for a long winter's nap,

When out on the lawn
there arose such a clatter,
I sprang from my bed
to see what was the matter.

Away to the window
I flew in a flash,
Tore open the shutters
and threw up the sash.

The moon on the breast
of the new-fallen snow
Gave a lustre of midday
to objects below,

When, what to my wondering
eyes should appear,
But a miniature sleigh
and eight tiny reindeer,

With a little old driver,
so lively and quick,
I knew in a moment
it must be St. Nick.

More rapid than eagles
his coursers they came,
And he whistled, and shouted,
and called them by name:

"Now, Dasher! now, Dancer!
now, Prancer and Vixen!
On, Comet! on, Cupid!
on, Donder and Blitzen!

To the top of the porch!
to the top of the wall!
Now dash away! dash away!
dash away, all!"

As dry leaves that before
the wild hurricane fly,
When they meet with an obstacle,
mount to the sky,

So up to the housetop
the coursers they flew,
With a sleigh full of toys,
and St. Nicholas, too.

And then, in a twinkling,
I heard on the roof
The prancing and pawing
of each little hoof.

As I drew in my head,
and was turning around,
Down the chimney St. Nicholas
came with a bound.

He was dressed all in fur,
from his head to his foot,
And his clothes were all tarnished
with ashes and soot;

A bundle of toys he had
flung on his back,
And he looked like a peddlar
just opening his pack.

His eyes – how they twinkled!
his dimples, how merry!
His cheeks were like roses,
his nose like a cherry!

His droll little mouth
was drawn up like a bow,
And the beard on his chin
was as white as the snow;

The stump of a pipe
he held tight in his teeth,
And the smoke, it encircled
his head like a wreath;

He had a broad face
and a little round belly
That shook, when he laughed,
like a bowl full of jelly.

He was chubby and plump,
a right jolly old elf,
And I laughed when I saw him,
in spite of myself;

A wink of his eye
and a twist of his head,
Soon gave me to know
I had nothing to dread;

He spoke not a word,
but went straight to his work,
And filled all the stockings;
then turned with a jerk,

And laying a finger
aside of his nose,
And giving a nod,
up the chimney he rose.

He sprang to his sleigh,
to his team gave a whistle,
And away they all flew
like the down of a thistle.

But I heard him exclaim,
ere he drove out of sight,
"Happy Christmas to all,
And to all a good night!"

CLEMENT CLARKE MOORE

Merry Christmas

God bless
the master of this house,
The mistress bless also,
And all the little children
that round the table go;
And all your kin and kinsmen,
That dwell both far and near:
I wish you Merry Christmas
And a Happy New Year!

CLEMENT
CLARKE
MOORE

Lullaby

Sweet and low, sweet and low,
Wind of the western sea,
Low, low, breathe and blow,
Wind of the western sea!

Over the rolling waters go,
Come from the dying moon and blow,
Blow him again to me;
While my little one, while my pretty one,
sleeps.

Sleep and rest, sleep and rest,
Father will come to thee soon;
Rest, rest, on mother's breast,
Father will come to thee soon;

Father will come to his babe in the nest,
Silver sails all out of the west
Under the silver moon:
Sleep, my little one; sleep, my pretty one,
sleep.

Alfred,
Lord Tennyson

Twinkle, Twinkle,
Little Star

Twinkle, twinkle, little star,
How I wonder what you are!
Up above the moon so high,
Like a diamond in the sky.

Jane Taylor

Matthew, Mark, Luke, and John

Matthew, Mark, Luke, and John,
Bless the bed
That I lie on!
Four corners to my bed,
Four angels round my head;
One to watch, One to pray,
And two to bear
My soul away!

Traditional

Cupboard Land

Good night, dear toys, we love you so,
But Mother's calling, we must go;
The day has been so sweet and bright,
So go to sleep till morning light.

Good night, dear Dolly, do not fear,
For good old Dobbin's watching near,
And now and then he'll give a bray,
And that will keep the ghosts away.

Good night, dear Dobbin, stay awake
And watch o'er Dolly for my sake;
Don't let her fear – you understand,
But keep good watch in Cupboard Land.

Good night, my dear old butcher's shop;
Good night, dear drum, and flag, and top;
When day returns we'll have such fun,
Good night, good night, to everyone!

FRED E. WEATHERLY

Escape at Bedtime

The lights from the parlour
and kitchen shone out
Through the blinds and
the windows and bars;
And high overhead
and all moving about,
There were thousands of
millions of stars.
There ne'er were such thousands
of leaves on a tree,
Nor of people in church or the Park,
As the crowds of the stars
that looked down upon me,
And that glittered
and winked in the dark.

The Dog, and the Plough,
and the Hunter, and all,
And the star of the sailor, and Mars,
These shone in the sky,
and the pail by the wall
Would be half full of water and stars.
They saw me at last,
and they chased me with cries,
And they soon had me packed into bed;
But the glory kept shining
and bright in my eyes,
And the stars going round in my head.

ROBERT LOUIS STEVENSON

North-West Passage

1. Good Night

When the bright lamp is carried in,
The sunless hours again begin;
O'er all without, in field and lane,
The haunted night returns again.

Now we behold the embers flee
About the firelit hearth; and see
Our faces painted as we pass,
Like pictures, on the window-glass.

Must we to bed indeed? Well then,
Let us arise and go like men,
And face with an undaunted tread
The long black passage up to bed.

Farewell, O brother, sister, sire!
O pleasant party round the fire!
The songs you sing, the tales you tell,
Till far tomorrow, fare ye well!

ROBERT LOUIS STEVENSON

Come to the Window

Come to the window,
My baby with me,
And look at the stars
That shine on the sea!
There are two little stars
That play bo-peep,

With two little fish
Far down in the deep;
And two little frogs
Cry neap, neap, neap;
I see a dear baby
That should be asleep.

Traditional

Good Night!
Good Night!

Good night! Good night!
Far flies the light;
But still God's love
Shall flame above,
Making all bright.
Good night! Good night!

VICTOR HUGO

The End